FRIENDLY PHYSICAL SCIENCE

TESTS

Note that a PDF version of these tests is available.

See our website for details on purchasing.

www.friendlyphysicalscience.com

Name_____ Date_____

Friendly Physical Science

Lesson 1 Test

Please read each question carefully. Choose the one best answer. Indicate your choice by circling the letter.

1. Physical science is the study of those things in our world which are

a. living

b. non-living

c. alive

d. from times past

2. The distance from one point to another is known as

a. mass

b. length

c. weight

d. very far

3. Measuring something means we are comparing an unknown quantity to a

a. unknown standard

b. list of known objects

c. known standard

d. known location of events

4. Which of the following units is not a member of the English system of measuring length?

a. meter

b. inches

c. feet

d. miles

5. The metric system is known as the SI. What does SI stand for?

a. System involvement

b. International metric system

c. International System

d. System Introversion

6. The metric system relies on the standard units being in multiples of

a. 50s

b. 10s

c. 3s

d. 20s

7. The base unit for length in the SI system is the

a. mass

b. gram

c. mile

d. meter

8. The base unit for mass in the SI system is the

a. gram

b. pound

c. ounce

d. meter

9. How many decimeters would you find in a meter?

a. 100

b. 1/10th

c. 10

d. none

10. There are _____ centimeters in a meter.

a. 15

b. 1000

c. 10

d. 100

11. How many milliliters might you find in a liter?

a. 100,000

b. 1000

c. 100

d. 10

12. If Tony traveled 200 kilometers on his bike, how many meters did he travel?

a. 2000

b. 200,000

c. 2

d. 3 miles

13. Look at the diagram below of a field of corn. If you needed to build a fence around the perimeter (outside edge) of the field, how many feet of fencing would be required?

a. 30 miles

b. 20 miles

c. 10 kilometers

d. 30 kilometers

10 kilometers

5 kilometers

Name_____ Date_____

Friendly Physical Science

Lesson 2 Test

Please read each question carefully. Choose the one best answer. Indicate your choice by circling the letter.

1. Measurements made when two or more base measurements are added, subtracted, multiplied or divided are known as

a. difficult to understand measurements

b. base measurements

c. derived measurements

d. non-standard measurements

2. The amount of space in a location is known as

a. mass

b. surface area

c. volume

d. cubic feet

3. Surface area is a _____ dimensional measurment because it is derived from two measurements.

a. one

b. two

c. three

d. four

4. A piece of carpeting has the following floor dimensions: 15 feet by 20 feet. What is the area of this piece of carpeting?

a. 35 feet

b. 300 feet

c. 300 square feet

d. 35 square feet

5. Another room in the house has the following dimensions: 32 feet by 20 feet. Would a rug with the area of 540 square feet be large enough to completely cover the floor?

a. yes

b. no

c. we need additional information regarding the carpet

d. no because the color of the carpet is not appealing

6. A field measures 800 feet long and has a width of 200 feet. What is the area of this field?

a. 1000 feet

b. 2000 feet

c. 160,000 square feet

d. 160,000 feet/square

7. Suppose you have 20 cows and each cow requires 10,000 square feet of pasture. What is the total size of the pasture you would need for your herd of cows?

a. 20,000 square feet

b. 19,000 square feet

c. 2000 square feet

d. 200,000 square feet

8. Referring back to question 7, suppose one side of your pasture measured 1000 feet. What must the other dimension be of the pasture to make sure all cows had enough area to graze?

a. 200 feet

b. 2000 feet

c. 20 feet

d. 1000 feet

Name_____ Date_____

Friendly Physical Science

Lesson 3 Test

Please read each question carefully. Choose the one best answer. Indicate your choice by circling the letter.

1. The amount of space something takes up in known as its

a. shape

b. volume

c. mass

d. rank

2. Volume is a

a. base measurement

b. derived measurement

c. deprived measurement

d. base estimation

3. A regularly-shaped object has surfaces which are

a. colorful

b. flat and shaped like a square or rectangle

c. bumpy and irregular

d. never flat

4. In order to find the volume of a regularly-shaped object one must first find the

a. volume of the base of the object

b. surface area of all six sides of the object

c. surface area of the bottom or base of the object

d. volume of the top of the object

5. After finding the area of the base of the object, this value is multiplied by the

a. height of the object

b. volume of the object

c. surface area of the base of the object

d. mass of the object

6. Volume measurements of regularly-shaped objects are in

a. square units

b. base units

c. units squared

d. cubic units

7. The "formula" for finding the volume of a regularly-shaped object, therefore, is to multiply the

a. length x width x height of the object

b. width x width x width

c. length x height x volume

d. length x width

8. Mary has a box with these dimensions: length = 4 cm; width = 5 cm and height = 10 cm. What is the volume of Mary's box?

a. 200 square centimeters

b. 150 cubic centimeters

c. 200 cubic centimeters

d. 30 cubic centimeters

9. Tony's object has a volume of 450 cubic centimeters. Francine's has the following dimensions: length = 4.5 cm, width = 10 cm and height = 10 cm. Who has the larger object?

a. Tony   c. They are the same size

b. Francine

Name_____ Date_____

Friendly Physical Science

Lesson 4 Test

Please read each question carefully. Choose the one best answer. Indicate your choice by circling the letter.

1. A measure of how much space an object occupies is

a. mass

b. shape

c. area

d. volume

2. Volume is a _____ dimensional measurement.

a. one

b. base

c. three

d. two

3. An irregularly-shaped object has surfaces which are not

a. happy

b. flat

c. bumpy

d. colorful

4. To find the volume of an irregularly-shaped object we can use the

a. displacement method

b. volumetric calibration method

c. length x width x height x mass

5. With regard to the displacement method of finding volume, the

a. volume of water displaced by the object equals the mass of the object

b. mass of the water displaced equals the mass of the object

c. volume of the water displaced by the object equals the volume of the object

d. the shape of the object determines if the object has volume or not

6. The SI unit for volume of an irregularly-shaped object is usually the

a. milliliter

b. centimeter

c. millimeter

d. cubic foot

7. A liter can be divided into 1000 equal parts. Each of these "little" parts are known as a

a. quart

b. gallon

c. millimeter

d. milliliter

8. The upper surface of a liquid placed into a graduated cylinder is curved in shape. This curve is known as the

a. equatorial line

b. meniscus

c. volumetric flask

d. line of no return

9. Bill dropped an irregularly-shaped object into a beaker with 100 mL of water. The water rose to 195 mL. What was the volume of Bill's object?

a. 295 mL

b. 100 mL

c. 90 mL   d. 95 mL

10. How many pints are in one quart?

a. four

b. two

c. sixteen

d. eight

11. If a gallon has 4 quarts and each quart has two pints, how many pints would there be in three gallons?

a. eight

b. eighteen

c. twelve

d. twenty four

Friendly Physical Science

Lesson 5 Test

Please read each question carefully. Choose the one best answer. Indicate your choice by circling the letter.

1. Mass the the amount of

a. matter in an object

b. space an object occupies

c. matter covering an object

d. force required to break an object

2. Mass and weight are not the same thing. This is a _____ statement (true or false).

a. true

b. false

3. Matter consists of small bits known as

a. futons

b. atoms

c. photons

d. croutons

4. Weight is dependent upon

a. size of the object

b. gravity

c. number of atoms in the object

d. how much you eat

5. Two instruments which can be used to measure mass are the

a. scale and graduated cylinder

b. scale and balance

c. measuring cup and balance

d. graduated cylinder and balance

6. The SI units for mass are

a. grams

b. pounds

c. ounces

d. meters

7. One thousand grams equal one

a. centigram

b. kilometer

c. milligram

d. kilogram

8. One one-thousandth of a gram equals one

a. centigram

b. kilometer

c. kilogram

d. milligram

9. There are _____ grams in one pound.

a. 1000

b. 395

c. 454

d. 0.1

10. One US ton equals _____ pounds.

a. 1000   c. 100

b. 2000   d. 200

Name_____ Date_____

Friendly Physical Science

Lesson 6 Test

Please read each question carefully. Choose the one best answer. Indicate your choice by circling the letter.

1. Density is the

a. amount of matter that can be found in a unit of volume.

b. time it takes to travel across the street

c. amount of volume in one gram of an object

d. result of multiplying length x width x height of an object

2. The units for density are usually

a. grams per cubic centimeter or milliliter

b. feet per second

c. grams per kilometer

d. grams per meter

3. Which object on this list would likely have the greatest density: lead fishing weight, plastic ping pong ball, styrofoam cube or wooden block?

a. lead fishing weight

b. plastic ping pong ball

c. styrofoam cube

d. wooden block

4. To find the density of an irregularly-shaped object one would need to find

a. its volume by displacement and its mass

b. its mass by displacement and its volume using a balance

c. its volume by multiplying its three dimensions

d. the density of an irregularly-shaped object is impossible to find

5. An object has the following measurements: mass = 100 grams; volume = 50 mL What might its density be?

a. 50 grams per mL

b. 2 grams/mL

c. 500 grams/mL

d. 150 grams/mL

6. Would the object in question #5 sink or float when placed into water?

a. sink

b. float

7. True or False: density can be used to separate substances.

a. true

b. false

8. Harold had an unknown piece of metal. He took some measurements and found it had a mass of 27 grams. When he placed it into 100 mL of water, the water rose to 110 mL. Based on these observations and the known information below, what might be the identify of this obejct?

a. aluminum

b. lead

c. gold

d. zinc

Densities of common metals: Aluminum: 2.7 g/cc   Lead:11.3 g/cc   Copper: 8.96 g/cc

Cesium: 1.93 g/cc   Silver: 10.5 g/cc   Gold: 19.3 g/cc   Platinum: 21.5 g/cc

Titanium: 4.5 g/cc   Zinc: 7.41 g/cc

9. Tim's object had a mass of 50 grams. It had a volume of 55 mL. Would his object likely sink or float if placed into water?

a. sink

b. float

Name_____ Date_____

Friendly Physical Science

Lesson 7 Test

Please read each question carefully. Choose the one best answer. Indicate your choice by circling the letter.

1. Objects which have a density greater than that of water will

a. sink when placed into water

b. float when placed into water

c. disolve when placed into water

d. melt when placed into water

2. Objects which have a density less than that of water will

a. swim frantically when placed into water

b. float when placed into water

c. sink to the bottom of the container of water

d. disolve when placed into water

3. The force which allows objects to float that would otherwise sink based upon their density is known as

a. buoyancy

b. high density

c. meniscus

d. volume aperture

4. Tommy has two boats: Boat A has a volume of 500 cc. Boat B has a volume of 600 cc. The mass of each boat is 400 grams. Which boat will float, A or B, both or neither?

a. boat A

b. boat B

c. both will float

d. both will sink

Name_____ Date_____

Friendly Physical Science

Lesson 8 Test

Please read each question carefully. Choose the one best answer. Indicate your choice by circling the letter.

1. Energy is defined as

a. the ability or capacity to do work

b. what you feel on a hot day

c. the ability to calculate density of unknown objects

d. the feeling you get have drinking an energy dring

2. Work is defined as

a. a change in position or location of an object which has mass

b. the energy consumed after moving an object

c. the level to which you aspire

d. the place you go on vacation

3. The energy produced from movement of machines is known as

a. chemical energy

b. mechanical energy

c. nuclear energy

d. sound energy

4. Potential energy is

a. energy of motion

b. stored energy or energy "waiting" to do work

c. always in motion

d. energy left over from kinetic energy

5. Which situation below depicts kinetic energy?

a. a compressed bed spring

b. a stretched rubber band

c. the string on a bow (of bow and arrow combination) when released

d. the water in the tank of a potty

6. When lye and water are mixed, a lot of heat is generated. This heat would be an example of

a. chemical energy

b. sound energy

c. mechnaical energy

d. acid energy

7. True or False: Energy can be converted from one type to another.

a. true

b. false

8. Consider a person swinging on a swing. At what point on the swing will the person have the greatest amount of potential energy?

a. at the top of the swing cycle just before heading downward

b. at the middle of the swing cycle closest to the ground

c. in between the top and bottom of the swing cycle

d. a person on a swing only posseses kinetic energy

9. A handwarmer consists of a plastic bag filled with two chemicals. When the two chemicals get mixed, heat is given off. This is a great example of

a. a physical reaction

b. chemical energy

c. conversion of mechanical energy into light energy

d. how to keep cool on a hot day

Name_____ Date_____

Friendly Physical Science

Lesson 9 Test

Please read each question carefully. Choose the one best answer. Indicate your choice by circling the letter.

1. The base unit for time is the

a. minute

b. hour

c. day

d. second

2. One minute equals

a. 60 seconds

b. 3600 seconds

c. a long time when you're waiting

d. 1/60th of a day

3. One hour equals

a. 3600 seconds

b. 24 hours

c. 1 day

d. 60 seconds

4. Speed an be defined as the

a. distance required to travel a certain speed.

b. time it takes to weigh out a certain amount of mass

c. time it takes to travel a specified distance

d. time it takes to eat a candy bar

5. The mathematical formula for speed is

a. distance / time

b. time/ distance

c. seconds / length

d. distance / length

6. Units for speed utilized by automobiles in the US are

a. feet per second

b. miles per kilometer

c. miles per hour

d. meters per second

7. A measure of speed which includes the direction of travel is

a. velocity

b. acceleration

c. pitch

d. deceleration

8. A change in the rate of speed is known as

a. acceleration

b. speed

c. turning

d. timing

9. Hank traveled 80 meters in four seconds. How many meters per second was he traveling?

a. 2 meters per second

b. 4 meters per second

c. 20 meters per second

d. 40 meters per second squared

Name_____Date_____

Friendly Physical Science

Lesson 10 Test

Please read each question carefully. Choose the one best answer. Indicate your choice by circling the letter.

1. Newton's first law of motion states that an object

a. in motion travels at a greater speed when moving downhill than traveling uphill

b. in motion continues in motion in a straight line until acted upon by a force

c. will be acted upon by a force to change its direction of travel

d. acted upon by gravity will have the same mass in any location

2. A person is sitting in a car at a stop light. As the light turns green, the car moves away and the person's body is pressed into the seat of the car. This is an example of

a. Newton's first law which says objects at rest stay at rest until acted upon by a force.

b. Newton's first law which says objects always stay at rest even if acted upon by a force.

c. Newton's second law which says objects accelerate at rates which variable.

d. Newton's third law which says all forces have an equal and opposite force.

3. The term which describes objects in regard to Newton's first law is

a. momentum

b. speed

c. inertia

d. velocity

4. Newton's second law of motion tells of the relationship between

a. mass and acceleration

b. mass and weight

c. length and mass

d. length and acceleration

5. Newton's second law of motion says that as a force is applied to an object, its potential _____ will be amplified.

a. acceleration

b. direction of travel

c. gravity

d. mass

6. Newton's third law of motion states

a. for every force there is an equal, but opposite force at play

b. obejcts in motion remain in motion until an equal force comes into play

c. objects at rest remain at rest until acted upon by anothcr objcct

d. objects at rest remain at rest until acted upon by another force

7. Pushing a paddle against water to propel a boat forward is a good example of

a. Newton's first law of motion

b. Newton's second law of motion

c. Newton's third law of motion

d. Newton's fourth law of mtion

Name_____ Date_____

Friendly Physical Science

Lesson 11 Test

Please read each question carefully. Choose the one best answer. Indicate your choice by circling the letter.

1. A simple machine which consists of a straight bar or rod and a fulcrum is a

a. lever

b. wheel and axle

c. pulley

d. wedge

2. The point on which the bar or rod of a lever moves is the

a. effort arm

b. fulcrum

c. load arm

d. point of no return

3. There are two arms of a lever. The arm where an external force is being applied to the lever is known as the

a. load arm

b. effort arm

c. fulcrum

d. long arm

4. A lever where the fulcrum is placed between the effort arm and the load arm is classified as a

a. first class lever

b. second class lever

c. third class lever

d. fourth class lever

5. The magnification of a force using a simple machine such as a lever is known as

a. force enhancement

b. force magnification

c. work assistance

d. mechanical advantage

6. There are two ways to increase the mechanical advantage of a first class lever. Those ways are to

a. increase the length of the load arm or decrease the length of the effort arm

b. increase the length of the effort arm or increase the length of the load arm

c. increase the length of the effort arm or decrease the length of the load arm

d. shorten the effort arm and remove the load arm

7. A second class lever differs from a first class lever in that

a. the direction of travel of the object is the same as the direction of force that is being applied.

b. there is no effort arm in a second class lever

c. the effort arm is always shorter than the load arm in a second class lever

d. the load arm of a second class lever never moves

8. While both first and second class levers can provide a mechanical advantage for the user, the disadvantage of both is that

a. the distance the object moves is always more than the distance that the point of effort moves

b. the distance the object moves is always less than the distance the lever moves where the effort is being applied

c. the length of the effort arm is never long enough on each type of lever to really make any difference

d. there is no real disadvantage of these levers

9. The third class lever

a. provides a greater mechanical advantage for the user beyond the capaibilites of first or second class levers

b. provides no mechanical advantage for the user, but increases the speed at which the object moves

c. provides 4-5 times the mechanical advantage in every use of its type

d. provides minimal mechanical advantage for the user and should not be used for most situations

10. A broom is a great example of a

a. first class lever

b. second class lever

c. third class lever

d. fourth class lever

11. Suppose you had a pair of bolt cutters which utilized two sets of levers to do the job for you. If the first lever where your force is intially applied provides a mechanical advantage of 50 and the second lever, if used alone, provides a mechanical advantage of 10, what would be the total mechanical advantage of this system of levers?

a. 60

b. 75

c. 250

d. 500

Name_____ Date_____

Friendly Physical Science

Lesson 12 Test

Please read each question carefully. Choose the one best answer. Indicate your choice by circling the letter.

1. In a wheel and axle simple machine, how are the components identified?

a. the wheel has larger diameter while the axle has the smaller diameter

b. the wheel has the smaller diameter while the axle has the larger diameter

c. the components have similar diameters, it's the colors that allow you to tell the difference

d. the wheel component is where the force is always applied

2. What feature in a wheel and axle system determines the potential mechanical advantage of the system?

a. the length of the axle versus the thickness of the wheel

b. the difference in diameter between the axle and wheel

c. the color of each component

d. the shape of each component

3. When an effort force is applied to the _____ component of the wheel and axle system. a mechanical advantage is realized.

a. wheel

b. axle

4. In which wheel and axle system is a mechanical advantage realized?

a. steering wheel of car

b. ferris wheel

c. motorized merry-go-round

d. fan blade on electric fan

5. True or False: Regardless of where the force is applied, a wheel and axle simple machine always creates a mechanical advantage for the user.

a. true

b. false

6. What is the advantage of applying a force to the axle component of a wheel and axle system?

a. you gain a mechanical advantage

b. you increase the speed of rotation

c. the change the direction of the force

d. you decrease the speed of rotation

7. The captain's wheel (steering wheel) of a ship allows the user to easily adjust the rudder of the ship with little effort. Why is this the case?

a. the captain's wheel has a diameter larger than that of of the shaft or axle which adjusts the rudder

b. the captain's wheel has a diameter smaller than that of of the shaft or axle which adjusts the rudder

c. the captain's wheel has a diameter equal to that of of the shaft or axle which adjusts the rudder

d. the captain's wheel creates a force less than that of the shaft on which it turning

8. If the effort force is being applied to the wheel in each system below, which system would provide the greatest mechancal advantage?

a. A

b. B

c. C

d. D

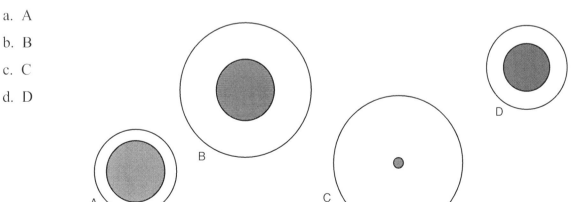

Name_____Date_____

Friendly Physical Science

Lesson 13 Test

Please read each question carefully. Choose the one best answer. Indicate your choice by circling the letter.

1. A pulley is similar to a wheel and axle system but differs in two ways. Those ways are

a. the pulley is attached to its axle and has a large diameter

b. the pully is not attached to its axle component and has a groove which allows a rope or chain to pass over it

c. the pulley is larger than most wheel and axle systems and has a groove to allow a rope or chain to pass

d. pulleys are not different from a wheel and axle system

2. If one pulls downward on a rope which is threaded through a single, fixed pulley the object to which the rope is tied will

a. move to a lower location

b. move to the left or right, but not upward

c. upward

d. in a circular fashion

3. A single fixed pulley system with one rope attached to the object

a. provides a means to change the direction of force applied to the object, yet provides no mechancial advantage for the user

b. provides a means to change the direction of force applied to the object and provides a mechancial advantage for the user of at least 2

c. provides no change the direction of force applied to the object and provides no mechancial advantage for the user

d. provides a mechanical advantage of more than 3 for the user of the system

4. What does adding pulleys do for a pulley system?

a. increases the expense at no gain to the user

b. increases the mechanical advantage for the user

c. decreases the amount of rope or chain necessary to raise or lower an object

d. decreases the mechanical advantage to the user

5. A multi-pulley system has four ropes which supports the lower, movable set of pulleys. What is the mechanical advantage of this pulley system?

a. 2

b. 3

c. 4

d. 5

6. The more pulleys you add to a pulley system may help in doing the work, but there is one big disadvantage. What is that big disadvantage?

a. Adding pulleys makes the pulley system take up more space.

b. Adding pulleys makes it harder to pull the rope through the pulleys.

c. Adding pulleys requires more rope to have to be pulled through the pulleys in order to lift the object.

d. Adding pulleys makes it more difficult to show someone how to do the work.

7. Pulleys can be joined together by belts to do work for us. Joining pulleys in this way allows us to

a. change the direction of rotation of a pulley

b. change the rate at which pulleys rotate

c. change the amount of force being applied to a pulley system

d. all of these are the possible results of linking pulleys together by belts

8. Consider the pulley system below. If a force is applied to pulley A, what can be said about pulley B?

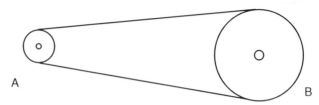

A

B

a. Pulley B will turn in the same direction as pulley A

b. Pulley B will turn more slowly than pulley A

c. Pulley B will provide a mechanical advantage for the user

d. All of the above responses are true regarding this pulley system

9. When pulleys are allowed to touch and have their surfaces engineered to have teeth and grooves, these pulleys are known as

a. gears

b. unsighltly pulleys

c. artificial pulleys

d. conveyors

10. Suppose you were riding a ten-speed bike and encountered a large hill. You wanted to bike up and then over the hill. To take advantage of your bike's capabilities, which option should you use; (1) a small gear as the pedal sprocket and large gear as the wheel sprocket or (2) a large gear at the pedal sprocket and a small gear at the wheel sprocket?

a. Option 1

b. Option 2

c. Either option will work as it will hard to get up the hill regardless of the gears you use.

Friendly Physical Science

Lesson 14 Test

Please read each question carefully. Choose the one best answer. Indicate your choice by circling the letter.

1. An inclined plane is a

a. circular surface affixed to a central axle

b. flat surface (plane) which has been raised or lifted on one end

c. a wavy surface

d. a rough surface

2. The mechanical advantage of an inclined plane is related

a. the rise and run of the ramp

b. the color of the ramp

c. the length of the ramp only

d. the rise of the ramp only

3. The longer the run of a ramp, the _____ the mechanical advantage of the ramp.

a. greater

b. lesser

4. A _____ is two inclined planes matched together.

a. wedge

b. gear

c. pulley

d. axle

5. If a wedge is being driven into a object in a vertical direction, what direction will this force be converted to?

a. horizontal

b. reverse vertical

c. north

d. upward

6. Choose the wedge with the greatest potential mechancal advantage.

Direction of effort force

A

B

C

D

a. wedge A

b. wedge B

c. wedge C

d. wedge D

7. An inclined plane wrapped around a central axis with a point on the end is known as a

a. screw

b bolt

c. nail

d. nut

8. Screws and bolts can convert

a. linear motion into straight motion

b. rotational motion into linear motion

c. rotational motion into circular motion

d. wedges into ramps

9. A(n) _____ is a screw which turns inside a cylinder and can be used to lift substances.

a. auger   b. bolt   c. pulley   d. sprocket

10. _____ is the reluctance of substances to move across each other when they are rubbed together. a. friction   b. motion   c. inertia   d. lubrication

Name_____ Date_____

Friendly Physical Science

Lesson 15 Test

Please read each question carefully. Choose the one best answer. Indicate your choice by circling the letter.

1. Pressure can be defined as
   a. the force between two surfaces
   b. a force acting in a perpendicular direction to a surface over a specific area
   c. the force of gravity acting within confined spaces
   d. the time it takes to deflate a ballon or ball

2. The SI units for pressure are
   a. Newtons
   b. Pascals
   c. Grams
   d. Square Meters

3. A pascal is
   a. one newton of force acting over 1 square meter of area
   b. one pound of force acting over 1 square foot of area
   c. one kilogram of force acting over 1 square centimeter of area
   d. one ounce of force

4. Pressure =
   a. force/foot
   b. force x area
   c. force / area
   d. area / force

5. Which substance is easier to compress?
   a. solids
   b. liquids
   c. gases

6. When pressure is applied to a liquid or gas that is in a closed container, the pressure is _____ distributed to all parts of the substance and therefore the pressure is equally felt upon all surfaces of the container.

a. not

b. unequally

c. never

d. equally

7. Two cylinders are connected by a hose to create a closed system. If you desired to create a mechanical advantage using these cylinders, what must be altered to achieve this goal?

a. Increase the amount of fluid or gas inside the system.

b. Adjust the diameter of the second cylinder to a larger size.

c. Decrease the diameter of the second cylinder.

d. Increase the length of hose between the cylinders.

8. True or false: gaining a mechanical advantage using a closed cylinder system comes at the expense of losing the distance traveled by the piston (plunger) of the second cylinder.

a. true

b. false

9. Systems which utlilze liquids to transfer forces through hoses and cylinders are known as
a. pneumatic systems
b. hydraulic systems
c. pressure captured systems
d. organic pressure systems

10. Systems which utilize gases to transfer forces through hoses and cylinders are known as
a. pneumatic systems
b. hydraulic systems
c. pressure captured systems
d. organic pressure systems

Name_____Date_____

Friendly Physical Science

Lesson 16 Test

Please read each question carefully. Choose the one best answer. Indicate your choice by circling the letter.

1. Magnetism is thought to occur due to

a. unidirectional spins of protons in magnetic substances

b. unidirectional spins of electrons in magnetic substances

c. unidirectional spins of neutrons in magnetic substances

d. bidirectional spins of electrons in magnetic substances

2. Magnets create three-dimensional

a. magnetic fields around them

b. electronic fields around them

c. bidirectional fields around them

d. unidirectional magnetic fields around them

3. "Like" magnetic poles of a magnet

a. repel each other

b. attract each other

4. "Unlike" magnetic poles _____ each other.

a. repel each other

b. attact each other

5. True or false: A non-magnetic substance can become magnetized by rubbing a permanent magnet across it repeatedly in the same direction.

a. true

b. false

6. Magnets which maintain their ability to attract or repel over long periods of time are known as

a. permanent magnets

b. horse shoe magnets

c. bar magnets

d. temporary magnets

7. Compasses work by

a. having their magnetic base respond to the magnetic field of the moon

b. having their magnetic base respond to the magnetic field of the earth

c. having their magnetic needle respond to the magnetic field of the earth

d. having their magnetic needle attract to the metal of the compass base

8. Examine the digram below of two magnets. Will these magnets attract or repel each other?

| N   S | | N   S |

a. repel each other
b. attract each other

Name_____ Date_____

Friendly Physical Science

Please read each question carefully. Choose the one best answer. Indicate your choice by circling the letter.

1. Electricity is the movement of

a. protons through substances

b. electrons through substances

c. neutrons through substances

d. croutons through salad

2. Electricity is found in two forms:

a. current and flowing

b. current and non-current

c. current and static

d. current and antistatic

3. Which statement below best describes DC electricity?

a. DC electricity is produced by batteries and flows in one direction through conductors

b. DC electricity is produced by generators and flows in two directions through conductors

c. DC electricity is produced by batteries and flows in two directions

d. DC electricity is produced by generators and flows in one direction

4. Which statement below best describes AC electricity?

a. AC electricity is produced by batteries and flows in one direction through conductors

b. AC electricity is produced by generators and flows in two directions through conductors

c. AC electricity is produced by batteries and flows in two directions

d. AC electricity is produced by generators and flows in one direction

5. Batteries create electricity

a. due to the turning of a turbine

b. due to the action of two similar metals and a basic substance

c. due to the reaction of two unlike metals and an acid

d. due to the reaction of an acidic and basic chemical

6. True or false: Metals, such as copper and aluminum, are great insulators because they allow electrons to readily flow through them.

a. true

b. false

7. Current is measured in

a. amps and is a measure of the strength of the electrical charge

b. volts and is a measure of the strength of the electrical charge

c. ohms and is a measure of the resistance of electrons to flow

d. amps and is a measure of the speed of flow of electrons

8. Voltage is measured in

a. amps and is a measure of the strength of the electrical charge

b. volts and is a measure of the strength of the electrical charge

c. ohms and is a measure of the resistance of electrons to flow

d. amps and is a measure of the speed of flow of electrons

9. Resistance is measured in

a. amps and is a measure of the strength of the electrical charge

b. volts and is a measure of the strength of the electrical charge

c. ohms and is a measure of the resistance of electrons to flow

d. amps and is a measure of the speed of flow of electrons

10. Which item below works to limit the flow of electricity to safe levels?

a. fuse

b. breaker switch

electrical outlet   d. choices a and b are both good answers

Name_____ Date_____

Friendly Physical Science

Lesson 18 Test

Please read each question carefully. Choose the one best answer. Indicate your choice by circling the letter.

1. Electromagnets work through the

a. presence of magnetic fields which occur around wires carring electricity

b. presence of electronic fields which occur around magnets

c. presence of magnetic fields which occur around metallic substances

d. presence of electrical currents produced by magnets

2. There are two components required to make an electromagnet. Those components are:

a. a wire carrying electricity and a switch

b. a wire carrying electricity and a soft iron metal rod or core

c. a permanent magnet and a soft iron metal core

d. a permanent magnet and a switch

3. Electromagnets differ from permanent magnets in that

a. electromagnets are much more expensive than permanent magnets

b. electromagnets can be turned on and off while permanent magnets are "on" all the time

c. electromagnets are always stronger than permanent magnets

d. electronmagnets are always weaker than permanent magnets

4. True or false: The polarity of an electromagnet can be reversed by reversing the flow of electricity making the magnet.

a. true

b. false

5. Two components are required for an electric motor to work. Which TWO from the list below are required:

a. permanent magnet   b. electromagnet   c. battery   d. switch

Name_____ Date_____

Friendly Physical Science

Lesson 19 Test

Please read each question carefully. Choose the one best answer. Indicate your choice by circling the letter.

1. Light is defined as the

a. visible spectrum of electromagnetic radiation which has the capability of traveling from place to place

b. non-visible spectrum of electromagnetic radiation what has no capability of traveling from place to place

c. energy created when mechanical forces create electrical visible electrical impulses

d. energy created from the exposure of magnetic fields to electrical fields

2. Light travels at approximately

a. 186,000 miles per second

b. 58,000 miles per second

c. 669,600 miles per second

d. 70,000 feet per second

3. Light that we can see is part of the

a. non-visible spectrum

b. visible spectrum

c. infrared spectrum

d. ultrviolet spectrum

4. Light travels in

a. waves

b. conductors

c. groups

d. buses

5. The wavelength of light determines the

a. speed of the light

b. shape of the light

c. color of the light we perceive

d. intensity of the light

6. When we see a red ball, this means that

a. the red wavelengths of light are being reflected to our eyes

b. the red wavelengths of light are being absorbed by the ball

c. all light is being absorbed by the ball

d. all light is being reflected by the ball

7. A device that can be used to separate light into the spectrum of wavelengths is the

a. telescope

b. microscope

c. lens

d. prism

8. Refraction is the

a. bending of light as it travels from one substance to another

b. bouncing of light off a surface

c. bending of light as it gets reflected off of surfaces

d. time it takes light to travel through a translucent substance

9. Lenses work by

a. refracting light

b. reflecting light

c. breaking light

d. interfering with the wavelength of light

Friendly Physical Science

Lesson 20 Test

Please read each question carefully. Choose the one best answer. Indicate your choice by circling the letter.

1. Sound energy travels in

a. waves

b. impulses

c. photons

d. buses, but not cars

2. Sounds are described as having a range of frequencies. Which statement below best describes these frequencies?

a. high frequency sound creates high pitches

b. high frequency sound creates low pitches

c. low frequency sounds are high pitched tones

d. low frequency sounds are unable to be heard by humans

3. True or false: Humans can hear a greater sprectrum of sound than all animals.

a. True

b. False

4. Which travels faster, light or sound?

a. light

b. sound

c. they travel at the same speed

5. Through which substance would sound travel the fastest?

a. wood block

b. milk

c. container of helium   d. bottle of water

8. Loudness of sound is measured in

a. decibels

b. pounds

c. ohms

d. waves

9. True or false: Loud sounds over long periods of time can damage one's ears.

a. true

b. false

10. Choose the sound below that would likely have the greatest decibel level.

a. rock concert

b. piano practice

c. dog barking

d. car horn

Friendly Physical Science

Lesson 21 Test

Please read each question carefully. Choose the one best answer. Indicate your choice by circling the letter.

1. Of the four stages of matter, which has the least amount of energy?

a. plasma

b. gases

c. liquids

d. solids

2. The temperature at which a solid changes to a liquid is known as the

a. melting point

b. boiling point

c. freezing point

d. flying point

3. The temperature at which a liquid changes to a gas is known as the _____ point or evaporation point.

a. boiling

b. melting

c. freezing

d. emulsification

4. Which scale listed below is not a measure of temperature?

a. Fahrenheit

b. Celsius

c. Kelvin

d. Decibel

5. Zero degrees Kelvin is known as _____ zero where all action of atoms in a substance ceases.

a. internal

b. exceptional

c. absolute

d. intensive

6. In general, most substances

a. expand when heated

b. contract when heated

c. expand when cooled

d. do not change size as temperature changes

7. A metal spoon sitting in a pot of simmering soup getting hot on the handle. This is an example of heat movement by

a. conduction

b. convection

c. radiation

d. contraction

8. Air moving up the stairs from a heated basement is an example of heat moving through

a. conduction

b. convection

c. contact

d. radiation

9. Unlike other substances, water _____ upon freezing.

a. expands

b. contracts

c. does not change   d. melts

Name_____ Date_____

Friendly Physical Science

Lesson 22 Test

Please read each question carefully. Choose the one best answer. Indicate your choice by circling the letter.

1. All things, whether living or not, are composed of tiny bits of matter known as:
a. Atoms
b. Crumbs
c. Propellant particles
d. Energized photons

2. The atomic theory says that atoms are composed of yet smaller subatomic particles. The subatomic particles found in the nucleus of the atom are the
a. Electrons and protons
b. Electrons and neutrons
c. Electrons
d. Protons and neutrons

3. The number of electrons found in an atom can be found on the periodic table of elements. This value is known as the:
a. Atomic mass number
b. Atomic number
c. Element symbol
d. Electron mass number

4. The arrangement of the _____ tells us about the behavior or reactivity of an element's atoms.
a. Protons
b. Neutrons
c. Electrons
d. Croutons

5. Which statement below is correct regarding the behavior of atoms of various elements?
a. Elements whose atoms have their outermost layer of protons completely filled are most stable.
b. Elements which have their nucleus filled with electrons are the most stable.
c. Elements which have their outermost layer of electrons partially filled are the most stable.
d. Elements which have their outermost layer of electrons completely filled are the most stable elements.

6. Elements which are unstable are able to gain stability by forming _____ with other unstable elements.
a. Business relationships.
b. Partnerships
c. Bonds
d. Stocks and mutual funds

7. When atoms transfer electrons from one to another in order to form greater stability, a(n) _____ bond is said have formed.
a. Ionic
b. Ironic
c. Covalent
d. Life-long

_____8. When atoms share electrons, rather than transfer electrons, to achieve greater stability, _____ bonds are said to have formed.
a. Ionic
b. Covalent
c. Neutronic
d. Savings

_____9. Oxygen atoms share two electrons and therefore the bond formed is called a:
a. Single ionic bond
b. Double ionic bond
c. Triple covalent bond
d. Double covalent bond

_____10. Four elements which are vitally important to living things are:
a. Carbon, hydrogen, helium and neon
b. Calcium, hydrogen, oxygen and nickel
c. Carbon, hydrogen, oxygen and nitrogen
d. Carbon, hydrogen, oxigen and nitrogin

FRIENDLY PHYSICAL SCIENCE

WORKSHEET SOLUTIONS

Name_____ Date_____

Friendly Physical Science

Lesson 1 Worksheet 1

Please fill in the missing words in each statement below. Refer back to your textbook for help.

1. Physical science is the study of those things in our world with are __NON-LIVING_.

2. ___MEASUREMENT___ is important in studying non-living things.

3. The distance from one point to another is known as __LENGTH____.

4. Measuring something means we are comparing an unknown quantity to a _STANDARD_ or known quantity.

5. Standards must be __AGREED UPON__ by those persons using it.

6. The English system of measurement utilizes ___INCHES__, ___FEET_____ and miles as the standard of length measurement.

7. The metric system is known as the SI or ____INTERNATIONAL SYSTEM___.

8. The metric system relies on the standard units being in multiples of ___TEN___.

9. The base unit for length in the SI system is the ____METER_____.

10. The base unit for mass in the SI system is the ____GRAM_____.

11. The base unit for time in the SI system is the _____SECOND_____.

12. The metric prefix deci- refers to _____1/10TH_____ of the base unit.

13. A decimeter is ____1/10TH_____ of a meter.

14. The metric prefix centi- refers to _____1/100TH_____ of the base unit.

15. A centimeter is _____1/100TH_____ of a meter.

16. The metric prefix milli- refers to _____1/1000TH_____ of the base unit.

17. A millimeter is _____1/1000TH_____ of a meter.

18. The metric prefix deca- refers to ____10_____ times the base unit.

19. A decameter equals _____10_____ meters.

20. The metric prefix hecto- refers to _____100_____ times the base unit.

21. A hectometer equals ___100____ meters.

22. The metric prefix kilo- refers to ___1000_____ times the base unit.

23. A kilometer equals ___1000_____ meters.

Name_____Date_____

Friendly Physical Science

Lesson 1 Worksheet 2

Below you will find 10 lines. Find the length of each line in the designated set of units.

1. _____ ____4___ inches

2. _____ ____2.5____ inches

3. _____ ____4.5____ inches

4. _____ ___1.75_____ inches

5. _____ ____1____ inch

6. _____
   __14____ cm

7. _____
   __11.5___ cm

8. _____
   _12.5____ cm

9. _____
   ____5____ cm

10. _____ ___11____ cm

Choose the best response to this question.

11. John had 40 decimeters of gold thread. Mary had 40 decameters of gold thread. Who had the longer piece of gold thread and why?

a. John had the longer piece because one decimeter is longer than one decameter.

b. John had the longer piece because one decameter is longer than one decimeter.

c. Mary had the longer piece because one decameter is longer than one decimeter.

d. Neither had a longer piece as one decimeter equals one decameter.

Name_____ Date_____

Friendly Physical Science

Lesson 2 Worksheet 1

Please fill in the missing words in each statement below. Refer back to your textbook for help.

1. Measurements made when two or more base measurements are added, subtracted, multiplied or divided are known as _____DERIVED_____ measurements.

2. The amount of space in a location is known as _____SURFACE AREA_____.

3. Surface area is a ____2____ dimensional measurment (derived from two measurements).

4. Floor tiles are usually ____1____ foot in length and width.

5. A floor tile measuring one foot in length and width is considered to have a surface area of _____1 SQUARE FOOT_____.

6. A room in a house has the following floor dimensions: 20 feet by 25 feet. What is the area of the floor of the room in this house? _____500 SQUARE FEET_____.

7. Another room in the house has the following dimensions: 32 feet by 20 feet. What is the area of the floor in this room? _____640 SQUARE FEET_____.

8. A field measures 800 feet long and has a width of 200 feet. What is the area of this field?

___160,000 SQUARE FEET_____.

9.   Suppose you have 20 cows and each cow requires 500 square feet of pasture. What is the total size of the pasture you would need for your herd of cows? __10,000 SUARE FEET___.

10. Referring back to question 9, suppose one side of your pasture measured 50 feet. What must the other dimension be of the pasture to make sure all cows had enough area to graze? _____200 FEET_____. Make a sketch of the pasture here if necessary to help you solve this question.

Name_____Date_____

Friendly Physical Science

Lesson 2 Worksheet 2

Tim and Sue had several cards in various sizes. Below you can see the measurements of
these cards. Of the two cards given, choose who (Tim or Sue) had the card with the greater
surface area. Write that person's name in the blank for each question.

1. Tim's card measured 6 inches by 5 inches. Sue's card measured 16 inches by 2 inches.

_____SUE_____had the card with greater surface area.

2. Tim's card measured 6 inches by 3 inches. Sue's card measured 4 inches by 5 inches.

_____SUE_____had the card with greater surface area.

3. Tim's card measured 16 inches by 5 inches. Sue's card measured 9 inches by 8 inches.

_____TIM_____had the card with greater surface area.

4. Tim's card measured 2.5 inches by 4 inches. Sue's card measured 3 inches by 3 inches.

_____TIM_____had the card with greater surface area.

5. Tim's card measured 72 inches by 5 inches. Sue's card measured 9 inches by 40 inches.

_____BOTH SAME SIZE!___had the card with greater surface area.

Take a look at the box pictured here. What would be the total surface area of this box?
Write the area of each surface in the spaces below. Then find the total surface area of the
box.

6. Side A = _____30 cm^2_____

7. Side B = _____24 cm^2_____

8. Side C = _____30 cm^2_____

9. Side D = _____24 cm^2_____

10. Side E = _____20 cm^2_____

11. Side F = _____20 cm^2_____

12. Total surface area = _____148 cm^2_____

13. Would a 150 cm^2 piece of paper cover this box?

_____YES!_____

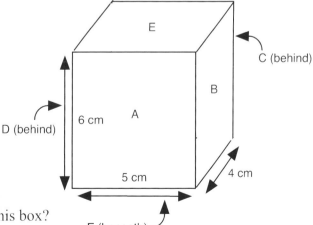

Name_____ Date_____

Friendly Physical Science

Lesson 3 Worksheet 1

Please fill in the missing words in each statement below. Refer back to your textbook for help.

1. The amount of space something takes up in known as its _____VOLUME_____.

2. Volume is a ____DERIVED____ measurement (base or derived?)

3. To find the volume of a regularly-shaped object, one must use the base measurement of ____LENGTH_____.

4. A regularly-shaped object has surfaces which are ___FLAT_____.

5. In order to find the volume of a regularly-shaped object one must first find the _____AREA_____ of the bottom or base of the object.

6. After finding the area of the base of the object, this value is multiplied by the _____HEIGHT_____ of the object.

7. Volume measurements of regularly-shaped objects are in ____CUBIC____ units or units^3.

8. The "formula" for finding the volume of a regularly-shaped object, therefore, is to multiply the _____LENGTH_____ times the _____WIDTH_____ times the _____HEIGHT____ of the object.

Examine each regularly-shaped object below. Find the volume of each.

9. ___60 cm^3___

10. ___44 cm^3____

11. ____200 cm^3___

12. ___176 cm^3____

9.

10.

5 cm

2 cm

11 cm

2 cm

4 cm

3 cm

11.

12.

3 cm

6 cm

2 cm

8 cm

8 cm

8 cm

4 cm

5 cm

10 cm

5

Name_____ Date_____

Friendly Physical Science

Lesson 3 Worksheet 2

There are ten regularly-shaped objects below. Match each shape to its measured volume.

1. Shape letter __J__ = ___64 cm³____
2. Shape letter __I__ = ___252 cm³___
3. Shape letter __H__ = ___216 cm³_
4. Shape letter __G__ = __105 cm³___
5. Shape letter __E OR F_ = ___175 c
6. Shape letter _E OR F_ = _175 cr
7. Shape letter _D__ = _72 cm³_
8. Shape letter _C__ = _36 cm³__
9. Shape letter __B__ = _100 cm³_
10. Shape letter _A__ = 80 cm³

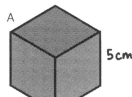
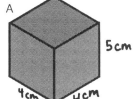
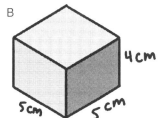
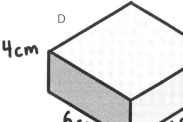
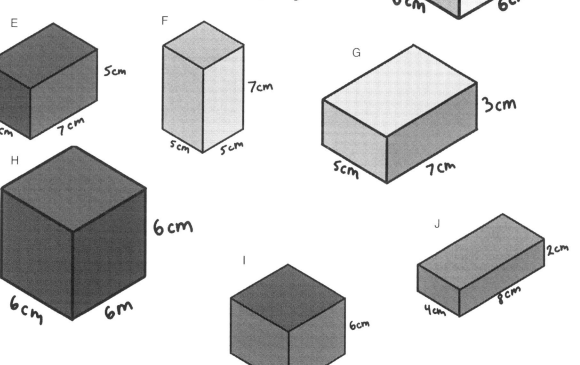

Name_____ Date_____

Friendly Physical Science

Lesson 4 Worksheet 1

Please fill in the missing words in each statement below. Refer back to your textbook for help.

1. ___VOLUME___ is a measure of how much space an object occupies.

2. Volume is a ___THREE___ dimensional measurement.

3. An irregularly-shaped object has surfaces which are not ____FLAT_____.

4. To find the volume of an irregularly-shaped object we can use the __DISPLACELMENT___ method.

5. With regard to the displacement method of finding volume, the ___VOLUME___ of water displaced by the object equals the ___VOLUME_____of the object.

6. The SI unit for volume of an irregularly-shaped object is the ____mL or cc_____.

7. A liter can be divided into 1000 equal parts. Each of these "little" parts are known as a _____MILLILITER_____ .

8. An instrument often used to find the volume of a liquid is the____GRADUATED___cylinder.

9. A milliliter of water equals 1 _____CC OR CUBIC CM_____ of water.

10. Syringes often measure liquids in _____CCs_____ (units).

11. The upper surface of a liquid placed into a graduated cylinder is ____CURVED___ in shape. This curve is known as the ____MENISCUS_____.

12. The rule to reading the volume of a liquid in a gradutted cylinder it to read the __BOTTOM___ of the meniscus.

13. __FOUR___ quarts are found in one gallon.

14. ___TWO___ cups are found in one pint.

15. ____TWO____ pints are found in one quart.

16. One cup contains _____EIGHT____ ounces.

17. ___THREE___teaspoons are found in one tablespoon.

18. _SIXTEEN_ cups are found in one gallon.

19. __SIXTY-FOUR__ cups are found in four gallons.

20. Ten tablespoons are found in __FIVE__ ounces.

Name_____ Date_____

Friendly Physical Science

Lesson 4 Worksheet 2

Read each scenario below and tell which of the two objects being measured is the larger of the two.

1. A container of water was filled to the 100 mL level. Object A was dropped in and the water rose to 150 mL. Object A was removed from the container. The water was refilled to the 90 mL level, object B was dropped in and the water rose to 130 mL. Which object was the larger of the two?

_____A_____

2. A container of water was filled to the 110 mL level. Object A was dropped in and the water rose to 115 mL. Object A was removed from the container. The water was refilled to the 120 mL level, object B was dropped in and the water rose to 130 mL. Which object was the larger of the two?

_____B_____

3. A container of water was filled to the 150 mL level. Object A was dropped in and the water rose to 185 mL. Object A was removed from the container. The water was refilled to the 110 mL level, object B was dropped in and the water rose to 145 mL. Which object was the larger of the two or are they the same?

_____THEY ARE THE SAME_____

4. A container of water was filled to the 125 mL level. Object A was dropped in and the water rose to 150 mL. Object A was removed from the container. The water was refilled to the 90 mL level, object B was dropped in and the water rose to 130 mL. Which object was the larger of the two?

_____B_____

Name_____ Date_____

Friendly Physical Science

Lesson 5 Worksheet

(Note: there is only one worksheet for Lesson 5)

Please fill in the missing words in each statement below. Refer back to your textbook for help.

1. Mass the the amount of _____MATTER___ in an object.

2. Mass and weight are not the same thing. This is a __TRUE__ statement (true or false).

3. Matter consists of small bits known as ___ATOMS____.

4. Weight is dependent upon ___GRAVITY OR LOCATION____.

5. An object's mass on the earth will __NOT__ change if it goes to the moon.

6. An object's weight __WILL__ change if it goes to a location where gravity is not the same.

7. The mass of an object is measured using a ___SCALE_____ or a _____BALANCE___.

8. The SI units for mass are ____GRAMS_____.

9. One thousand grams equal one ____KILOGRAM_____.

10. One one-thousandth of a gram equals one ___MILLIGRAM_____.

11. The English measurement for mass is the ____POUND_____.

12. One pound equals ___SIXTEEN__ dry ounces.

13. There are _____454____ grams in one pound.

14. One ton equals _____2000_____ pounds.

15. A metric ton equals ____1000____ kilograms.

Name_____ Date_____

Friendly Physical Science

Lesson 6 Worksheet 1

Please fill in the missing words in each statement below. Refer back to your textbook for help.

1. ___DENSITY___ is the amount of matter that can be found in a unit of volume.

2. The unit of volume usually associated with a density measurement is the __CUBIC CM___.

3. Density is a __DERIVED__ measurement (base or derived).

4. To find the density of an object one must first measure its ____MASS___ and then its _____VOLUME_____.

5. Lead fishing weights will have a ____GREATER___ density when compared to cotton balls.

6. If the object in which you would like to find the density is a regularly-shaped object, you could find its volume by __MULTIPLYING LENGTH X WIDTH X HEIGHT OF THE OBJECT___.

7. If the object in which you would like to find the density is an irregularly-shaped object, you could find its volume using the ___DISPLACEMENT____ method.

8. To find the mass of this object, you could use a __SCALE___ or ___BALANCE__.

9. The units for density would be ___GRAMS____ per __CUBIC CM____.

10. The density of pure water is ___1.0 GRAM/CUBIC CM (CC)_____.

11. Substances with a density greater than that of water will __SINK___ when placed into water.

12. Substances with a density less than that of water will __FLOAT___ when placed into water.

13. Density can be used to ___IDENTIFY OR SEPARATE____ substances.

14. Liquids, with varying __DENSITIES___ will separate, too.

15. The property of density can also be used to _____SEPARATE OR IDENTIFY____ substances.

Name_____ Date_____

Friendly Physical Science

Lesson 6 Worksheet 2

Francis had six unidentified pieces of metal. She thought that if she could determine the density of each piece, she might be able to figure out the identity of each piece using a reference book which told the accepted density of metals. She tested each piece of metal and took the average mass and volume. Those results are listed below. At the bottom of the page is a reference chart which tells accepted densities of various metals. Using Francis' results and the chart below, tell what you think the identity is for each unknown metal.

Sample 1: Mass 27.0 g Volume 10 cc Identity: _____2.7 g/cc Aluminum_____

Sample 2: Mass 44.5 g Volume 5 cc Identity: _____8.9 g/cc Copper_____

Sample 3: Mass 70.8 g Volume 12 cc Identity: _____5.9 g/cc Gallium_____

Sample 4: Mass 183.4 g Volume 9.5 cc Identity: _____19.3 g/cc Gold_____

Sample 5: Mass 215 g Volume 10 mL Identity: _____21.5 g/cc Platinum_____

Sample 6: Mass 147 g Volume 14 mL Identity: _____10.5 g/cc Silver_____

Metal Densities:

Aluminum: 2.7 g/cc   Lead:11.3 g/cc   Copper: 8.96 g/cc   Gallium: 5.91 g/cc

Cesium: 1.93 g/cc   Silver: 10.5 g/cc   Gold: 19.3 g/cc   Platinum: 21.5 g/cc

Titanium: 4.5 g/cc   Zinc: 7.41 g/cc

Name_____ Date_____

Friendly Physical Science

Lesson 7 Worksheet

(Note: there is only one worksheet for Lesson 7)

Please fill in the missing words in each statement below. Refer back to your textbook for help.

1. Objects which have a density greater than that of water will ___SINK____ when placed into water.

2. Objects which have a density less than that of water will ___FLOAT____ when placed into water.

3. The force which allows objects to float that would otherwise sink based upon their density is known as __BUOYANCY_____.

4. Increasing the volume of water being displaced while keeping the mass of an object constant can have the effect of reducing that object's ___density_____thereby enabling it to float.

5. Tommy has two boats: Boat A has a volume of 500 cc. Boat B has a volume of 600 cc. The mass of each boat is 400 grams. Which boat will float, A or B, both or neither?

_____BOTH_____

Name_____ Date_____

Friendly Physical Science

Lesson 8 Worksheet

(Note: there is only one worksheet for Lesson 8)

Please fill in the missing words in each statement below. Refer back to your textbook for help.

1. __ENERGY__ is defined as the ability or capacity to do work.

2. Work is defined as a change in ____POSITION___ of an object which has mass.

3. Energy can be present in various forms such as: __HEAT__, __MECHANICAL__, ___CHEMICAL___, ____SOUND/LIGHT____ or nuclear.

4. ____POTENTIAL____ energy is stored energy or energy "waiting" to do work.

5. ___KINETIC_____ energy is the energy of motion.

6. A shining light bulb could be an example of ____LIGHT____ or ___HEAT____ energy.

7. A pump with handle that can be moved up and down is an example of using ____MECHANICAL_____ energy to do work.

8. A beating drum creates _____SOUND____ energy.

9. Mixing various chemicals together can potentially produce __CHEMICAL___ energy.

10. Burning wood produces ____HEAT/LIGHT/SOUND____ energy.

11. True or False: Energy can be converted from one type to another. ___TRUE__

12. A compressed spring is an example of ___POTENTIAL____ energy.

13. A released spring flying through the air is an example of __POTENTIAL___ energy having been converted into ____KINETIC____ energy.

14. Water held behind a dam is an example of ___POTENTIAL_____ energy.

15. Water flowing through an outlet of a dam causing a turbine to turn is an example of potential energy being converted into ____KINETIC___ energy.

Name_____ Date_____

Friendly Physical Science

Lesson 9 Worksheet 1

Please fill in the missing words in each statement below. Refer back to your textbook for help.

1. The base unit for time is the ___SECOND____.

2. ___SIXTY___ seconds equals one minute.

3. ___SIXTY___ minutes or ____3600____ seconds equals one hour.

4. ___86,400___ seconds or ___1440___ minutes or _24___hours equals one day.

5. Speed can be defined as the ___TIME__ it takes to travel a specific __DISTANCE___.

6. The mathematical formula for speed is ___SPEED = DISTANCE/TIME_____.

7. The speed at which an automobile travels is usually measured in __MILES/HOUR____ in the US.

8. ___VELOCITY___ is also a measure of speed but it also includes the direction of travel.

9. A change in the rate of speed is known as ____ACCELERATION_____.

10. Speeding up is known as ____POSITIVE____ acceleration while slowing down is referred to as ___NEGATIVE____ acceleration.

Name_____Date_____

Friendly Physical Science

Lesson 9 Worksheet 2

Here are some story problems related to speed. Read each one carefully.

1. Tony traveled a distance of 500 feet on his bike in 40 seconds. How many feet per second was he traveling? _____12.5 FT/SEC_____

2. Marcus shot a bottle rocket into the sky. If it traveled 30 meters in three seconds, what as the speed of the rocket? _____10 M/SEC_____

3. Hank traveled 50 meters in 5 seconds. Marcia traveled 100 meters in 10 seconds. Who had the greater speed? _____SAME SPEED 10 M/SEC_____

4. Suppose you were in your car traveling at a speed of 60 miles per hour. If you were able to maintain that speed constantly for three hours, how far could you theoreticallly travel?

_____60 MILES EACH HOUR; 60 X 3 = 180 MILES_____

5. Mary was slowing down to make a left turn at a street intersection. Initially, she was traveling at 35 miles/hour. At the point of the turn, she was now travling at a speed of 10 miles/hour. Was Mary experiencing positive or negative acceleration as she made the turn?

____NEGATIVE___

Name_____ Date_____

Friendly Physical Science

Lesson 10 Worksheet 1

Please fill in the missing words in each statement below. Refer back to your textbook for help.

1. Newton's Three Laws of Motion can be credited to _ISAAC NEWTON____, however __GALILEO GALILEI____ and __RENE_DESCARTES____ had also made contributions to many of these ideas.

2. Newtons first law of motion states that an object in ___MOTION___ remains ___MOTION____ in a _____STRAIGHT____ line until acted upon by another ____FORCE___.

3. The force which could possibly be applied may change the object's ___DIRECTION____ of travel or _____RATE_____ speed of travel.

4. Newton's first law applies also to objects at ___REST____ in that an object at _REST__ will remain at ___REST_____ until acted upon by another force.

5. The term which describes objects in regard to Newton's first law is __INERTIA_____.

6. Newton's second law of motion tells of the relationship between ___FORCE_____, __MASS____ and ____ACCELERATION___.

7. Essentially, Newton's second law of motion says that as a force is applied to an object, its potential ____ACCELERATION____ will be amplified.

8. Newton's third law of motion states for every _____FORCE_____ there is an equal, but opposite ___FORCE_____.

9. Good examples of Newton's third law include ____ROWING____ a boat or walking across a ____FLOOR_____.

10. The _____BRAKES_____ in your car is a great example of how an object can apply a force to a moving object which results in a change in acceleration of that object.

Name_____Date_____

Friendly Physical Science

Lesson 10 Worksheet 2

Below are some "thinking" type questions. Read each question carefully and ALL possible responses. Choose the one best response to each question.

1. Harrison and Sheila were traveling on a gokart at a speed of 40 mph. Suddenly a rabbit ran out onto the gokart track in front of the two and Harrison hit the brakes very hard. Both Harrison and Sheila moved quite far forward onto the edge of the seat before their seatbelts applied a force to them. Why did they move forward even though the gokart was coming to a stop?

a. Both Harrison and Sheila were in motion before the rabbit ran out. The rabbit applied a magnetic force to the two causing them to move forward.

b. Both Harrison and Sheila were at rest in the car when the rabbit ran out in front of them. The braking of the gokart caused them to move forward.

c. Harrison and Sheila were both in motion when the brakes were being applied. They continued in motion according to Newton's first law of motion until the seatbelts applied a force to stop them.

d. Harrison and Sheila applied a force to the rabbit using the brakes of the car to teach it a lesson to not run across the road.

2. Marty was flying in an airplane for the very first time to visit his grandparents. As the plane was taking off, Marty felt his head and body being pressed into the seat, but later it lessened as the plane moved into the air. Why did this happen?

a. Marty was traveling at a slow speed as the plane taxied on the airstrip just before the plane quickly accelerated to a much faster speed for takeoff. His body desired to stay at the initial speed, but because the plane applied a greater force through the seat, he was moved into the seat.

b. Air in front of Marty quickly forced him to move forward to allow the plane to speed up for takeoff.

c. Marty's seat applied an upward force just before takeoff through a potential energy system found in the springs of the seat.

d. The force being applied to Marty cannot be explained.

3. Lisa and her friends liked to ride the super fast roller coasters at amusement parks. They

loved the thrill of suddenly going down a steep hill but knew it was important to not have any loose objects with them in the car of the roller coaster. Why is this important?

a. Newton's first law applies to all objects moving in the roller coaster car. A sudden turn or drop could result in those objects continuing in a straight line and being hurled out of the car.

b. Loose objects can make it difficult to keep one's feet firmly planted in the car of the roller coaster.

c. Newton's first law says that objects in motion always stop being in motion no matter how fast they are going to being with.

d. It's easy to hold onto loose objects while riding on a roller coaster, so it's always okay to just set them beside you on the seat and enjoy the ride.

4. Large semitrucks are often used to haul cattle to and from pastures or feedlots and slaughterhouses. The cattle are placed into large trailers, many times in two layers. The total weight of the cattle can often exceed 50,000 pounds. Which factor below must be considered when hauling such large loads of objects which are not using seatbelts?

a. Drivers must be careful to apply brakes slowly and in plenty of time to stop at intersections. Otherwise cattle may suddenly lurch forward causing the driver to have difficulty stopping the truck.

b. Drivers must be careful to make turns gradually at speeds much slower than in a personal automobile.

c. Drivers must be aware that the livestock can readily shift in position at unexpected times which may cause him to potentially lose control of the truck.

d. All of these factors are important to consider when hauling objects which can readily move around in a trailer.

Name_____Date_____

Friendly Physical Science

Lesson 11 Worksheet 1

Please fill in the missing words in each statement below. Refer back to your textbook for help.

1. __WORK__ is defined as the movement of an object through the action of a force.

2. __SIMPLE MACHINES___ allow us to do work on objects with less effort. They, in effect, "do" work for us.

3. _____LEVERS_____ are simple machines which consist of a straight bar or rod and a fulcrum.

4. The __FULCRUM___ is the point on which the bar or rod moves.

5. The rod or bar of a lever can be divided into two parts: the ___EFFORT_____ arm and the __LOAD__ arm.

6. The effort arm of a lever is where a force is ___APPLIED___ while the load arm is where a force is applied to an __OBJECT___.

7. Levers can be placed into three different ___CLASSES___ based upon where the ___FULCRUM___ is located.

8. A lever where the fulcrum is placed between the effort arm and the load arm is classified as a _____FIRST____class lever.

9. In a first class lever, the direction of the effort force is ___OPPOSITE___ that of the load force. In other words, if one presses down on a first class lever, the object being moved goes ___UP_____.

10. The magnification of a force using a simple machine is known as ___MECHANICAL ___ _____ADVANTAGE__.

11. To increase the mechanical advantage of a first class lever, one can either _____LENGTHEN____ the effort arm or ____SHORTEN_____ the load arm.

12. A ____SECOND____ class lever has the fulcrum beyond both the effort and load arms.

13. With a second class lever, both the __EFFORT___ force and the ___LOAD____ force move in the same ____DIRECTION____.

14. A ____TRAVOIS____ is an example of a second class lever that was used by Native Americans before the advent of wheeled carts or wagons.

15. Both class __1_____ and class _____2____ levers provide a mechanical advantage for the user, but the distance the object is moved is less than that of the effort distance.

More on the next page.

16. The ___EFFORT___ force is applied ____BETWEEN____ the fulcrum and the load in a third class lever sytem.

17. A third class lever system does not provide a __MECHANICAL ADVANTAGE__ for the user. Instead, it works to _____INCREASE_____ the speed of motion of the object upon which the force is being applied.

18. A __BROOM____ used to sweep or an ___OAR_____ used to paddle with are great examples of third class levers.

19. When levers are designed to work together, the force being applied is __MULTIPLIED__ from one lever to the next.

20. A __BOLT CUTTER__ used to cut bolts, heavy chains or locks is a great example of using multiple levers to make very difficult job very easy.

Name_____Date_____

Lesson 11 Worksheet 2

Below are some simple lever designs. Answer the questions about each of these designs to the best of your ability.

1. If a load is placed at point B and an effort force is applied downward at point A, in which direction will the load move?

<u>a. up</u>

b. down

c. left

d. north

2. If the load remains at point B, at what point would one gain the greatest mechanical advantage using this system?

<u>a. A</u>

b. B

c. C

d. D

3. If the load were moved to point D on the lever, would be force to lift the load become easier or more difficult

<u>a. Easier</u>

b. More difficult

c. It would remain the same

4. Would moving the fulcrum closer to point B (assuming the load is at point B) make it easier or more difficult to lift the load at point B?

<u>a. Yes, easier</u>

b. No, not easier

5. Assume a load is placed at point D on this lever and an effort force is applied in an upward direction at point A. Will the load move up or down?

a. Up

b. Down

c. It won't move at all.

6. Which class of lever would this system depict?

a. First class lever

b. Second class lever

c. Third class lever

d. Science class lever

7. To make the job of lifting an object using this system easier, which position would be the best to lift an object, point C, D or B?

a. C

b. D

c. B

d. it doesn't matter

Name_____ Date_____

Friendly Physical Science

Lesson 12 Worksheet 1

Please fill in the missing words in each statement below. Refer back to your textbook for help.

1. The ___WHEEL____ and __AXLE___ consists of two circular, disk-shaped objects that are joined together.

2. Of the two components, the wheel has the ___GREATER___ diameter while the axle has the _____LESSER____ diameter.

3. As the ____AXLE____ turns so does the wheel.

4. The greater the difference in the diameter of the two components, the greater the ___MECHANICAL ADVANTAGE___ of the wheel and axle system.

5. When an effort force is applied to the __WHEEL__ component of the wheel and axle system. a mechanical advantage is realized.

6. An example of this arrangement is the ___STEERING WHEEL___ in a car.

7. It's much ____EASIER____ to change the direction of travel in a car by using the steering wheel compared to just turning the bolt to which the steering wheel is attached.

8. Another example of this arrangement of wheel and axle is in the steering system of ____SHIPS/BOATS_____ where the wheel is used to adjust the rudder.

9. When an effort force is applied to the axle component in a wheel and axle system, the mechanical advantage realized is less than _____ONE_____ .

10. This means that there is __LESS__ work gained when applying a force to the axle of the wheel and axle system compared to when an effort force is applied to the wheel.

11. The advantage of applying a force to the axle component of a wheel and axle system is that the _____RATE/SPEED_____ of rotation of the wheel is greater than that of the axle.

Name_____ Date_____

Friendly Physical Science

Lesson 12 Worksheet 2

Examine each set of wheel and axle systems below. Assume the effort force is being applied to the wheel in the system. Choose which of the two would provide the greatest mechanical advantage.

1. A.   B.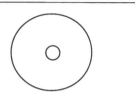

2. A. 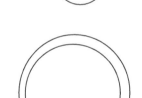   B.

3. A.   B.

4. A. 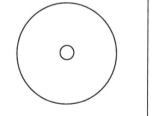   B.

Look at each wheel and axle system here. Assume the effort force is being appied to the axle. In which system would the wheel turn faster with one turn of the axle?

A.   B.

24

Name_____ Date_____

Friendly Physical Science

Lesson 13 Worksheet 1

Please fill in the missing words in each statement below. Refer back to your textbook for help.

1. A __PULLEY___ is similar to the wheel and axle simple machine in that it consists of a wheel and axle.

2. However, with a pulley, the wheel is __NOT___ attached to the axle. It, instead, ____TURNS_____ freely on the axle.

3. The wheel portion of a pulley has a groove on which a ___ROPE____ or __CHAIN___ can pass.

4. Pulleys allow one to ___CHANGE___ the ____DIRECTION___ of the force being applied to the object. If using a single fixed pulley, pulling ____DOWNWARD__ will move the object upward.

5. A single fixed pulley allows one to ___CHANGE__ the direction of force, however, it does not create any _____MECHANICAL_____advantage for the user.

6. A single, non-fixed pulley with its __TWO___ ropes or chains supporting the object can create a mechanical advantage of _____2_____ for the user.

7. By __ADDING____ more pulleys to a system of pulleys one can greatly increase the ___MECHANICAL ADVANTAGE____ of the system. The user's force can be ____MULTIPLIED_ many times.

8. A system of pulleys working side-by-side with a corresponding set of pulleys is known as a __BLOCK____ and ___TACKLE___.

9. The number of ropes or chains supporting the object in a block and tackle system tells you the ___MECHANICAL ADVANTAGE___ of the system.

10. For example, if you had four ropes supporting the object in a block and tackle system, the mechanical advantage would be _____4_____.

11. One disadvantage of a block and tackle system is that it requires ___LARGE_____ ___QUANTITES (GREAT LENGTHS)__ of rope or chain to lift an object. To combat this issue, this rope or chain can be "recycled" back into the system.

12. Pulleys can be joined together with other pulleys through the use of __CHAINS__ or ____BELTS_____. An example of this would be under the hood of your ____CAR____ where __BELTS____ transfer energy from the engine to other components requiring energy.

More on next page.

13. Pulleys that are joined through the use of belts or chains can __CHANGE___ the __DIRECTION_____ of the force being applied. In other words, a clockwise rotation can be converted to a ____COUNTERCLOCKWISE_____ rotation.

14. Pulleys that are joined through the use of belts of chains can also change the ____SPEED/RATE_____ of rotation.   A great example of this is a bike with several "speeds."

15. And, finally, pulleys that are joined together by a chain or belt can also be used to change the _____AMOUNT_____ of force one applies to the system.

16. ____GEARS____ are basically pulleys which have notched surfaces which match one another and come into contact with each other.

17. Like sets of pulleys linked with belts or chains, gears can also change the ___DIRECTION_____ of the force being applied, change the amount of the _____FORCE____ being applied or change the ___RATE/SPEEED_____ at which the initial gear is being turned.

Name_____Date_____

Friendly Physical Science

Lesson 13 Worksheet 2

Look at the systems of pulleys below. Answer the questions associated with each system.

1. What is the mechanical advantage of this pulley system?   2

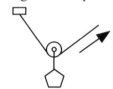

2. What is the mechanical advantage of this pulley system?   4

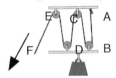

3. If pulley A is turning clockwise, what direction will pulley B turn?   CLOCKWISE

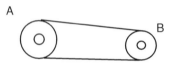

4. If pulley A is turning clockwise, what direction will pulley C turn?
COUNTERCLOCKWISE

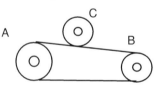

5. If pulley A makes one rotation, will pulley B make more or less rotations than pulley A?
MORE

6. If a force is being applied to sprocket A, will there be a mechanical advantage realized at sprocket B?   YES

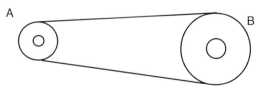

Name_____ Date_____

Friendly Physical Science

Lesson 14 Worksheet 1

Please fill in the missing words in each statement below. Refer back to your textbook for help.

1. An ___INCLINED PLANE_____ is a flat surface (plane) which has been raised or lifted on one end.

2. The mechanical advantage of a ramp is related to the ___LENGTH___ of the ramp (the run) and the ___HEIGHT_____ of the ramp (the rise).

3. The longer the run of a ramp, the _____GREATER_____ the mechanical advantage of the ramp.

4. A ___WEDGE___ is two inclined planes matched together.

5. Wedges are capable of changing the ___DIRECTION OF FORCE_____ being applied to the wedge.

6. The resulting direction of force is ___PERPENDICULAR____ to the initial force.

7. The mechanical advantage of a wedge is related to the ___LENGTH__ of the wedge and the _____ANGLE___ along the narrow edge of the wedge.

8. A ___SCREW_____ is an inclined plane wrapped into a circular shape. Screws and bolts convert ____CIRCULAR____ motion into ____LINEAR____ motion and, along with _____FRICTION____, can hold objects together.

9. An ____AUGER_____ is a screw which turns inside a cylinder and can be used to lift substances.

10. ____FRICTION_____ is the reluctance of substances to move across each other when they are rubbed together.

Name_____ Date_____

Friendly Physical Science

Lesson 14 Worksheet 2

Look at the systems of inclined planes below. Answer the question about each system.

1. Which ramp would provide the greater mechanical advantage?

2. Which ramp would provide the greater mechanical advantage?

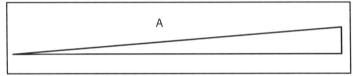 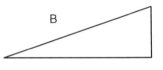

3. Which wedge would make your job easier?

 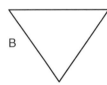

4. If this screw were turned in a clockwise direction, would it move into or out of this piece of wood? INTO

5. If you needed to lift a very heavy rock, which wedge would be your choice?

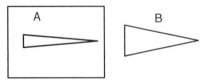

6. If this wedge were to be used to split this log, draw an arrow indicating the initial direction of force of the wedge and the resulting direction of force as it acted upon the log.

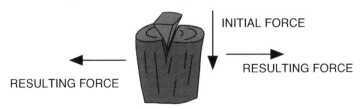

INITIAL FORCE

RESULTING FORCE

RESULTING FORCE

Name_____ Date_____

Friendly Physical Science

Lesson 15 Worksheet 1

Please fill in the missing words in each statement below. Refer back to your textbook for help.

1. _____PRESSURE___ can be defined as a force acting in a perpendicular direction to a surface over a specific __AREA_____.

2. Pressure is measured in SI units known as ____PASCALS___ (Pa). A pascal is defined as one ____NEWTON____ of force acting upon one __SQUARE METER__ of area.

3. Pressure = _____FORCE___/area. Pressure is the amount of ___FORCE_ per unit of area.

4. Liquids are very __DIFFICULT__to compress, however, gases can __EASILY__ be compressed.

5. When pressure is applied to a liquid or gas that is in a closed container, the pressure is __EQUALLY_ distributed to all parts of the substance and therefore the pressure is equally felt upon all surfaces of the container.

6. A mechanical advantage can be realized by adjusting the __SURFACE AREA_ upon which a pressure is acting in multi-cylinder systems.

7. An increase in mechanical advantage of a pressurized cylinder system comes at the cost of __DECREASING THE DISTANCE_____ traveled by second cylinder of the system.

8. Systems which utlize liquids to transfer forces through hoses and cylinders are known as ___HYDRAULIC__ systems.

9. Systems which utilze gases to transfer forces through hoses and cylinders are known as ___PNEUMATIC__ systems.

10. __PNEUMATIC_ systems tend to exhibit a "gentler" start at actuation while __HYDRAULIC___ tend to be more abrupt at actuation of the system.

Name_____Date_____

Friendly Physical Science

Lesson 15 Worksheet 1

Examine each pressure system below. Answer the question found with each system.

1. Cylinder A has a surface area of 4 cm². Cylinder B has a surface area of 8 cm². Will actuating Cylinder A provide a mechanical advantage for the user? If so, how much? YES, 2

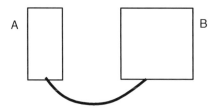

2. Cylinder A has a surface area of 4 cm². Cylinder B has a surface area of 16 cm². Will actuating Cylinder A provide a mechanical advantage for the user? If so, how much? YES, 4

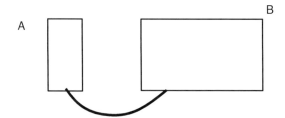

3. Cylinder A has a surface area of 4 cm². Cylinder B has a surface area of 2 cm². Will actuating Cylinder A provide a mechanical advantage for the user? If so, how much? NO

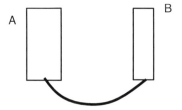

4. Suppose you wanted to utilize a hydraulic system to move a lever a great distance by moving the control lever only a short distance. Would you want the second cylinder to have larger or smaller diameter than the control lever? Why? SMALLER, AS IT WOULD MOVE A GREATER DISTANCE COMPARED TO THE DISTANCE MOVED BY THE CONTROL LEVER.

Name_____ Date_____

Friendly Physical Science

Lesson 16 Worksheet

(Note that Lesson 16 has only one worksheet.)

Please fill in the missing words in each statement below. Refer back to your textbook for help.

1. _____MAGNETISM_____ is thought to occur due to unidirectional spins of _____ELECTRONS____ in magnetic substances.

2. The term unidirectional means _____ONE DIRECTION____ .

3. Magnets create three-dimensional __MAGNETIC_ __FIELDS___ about them.

4. "Like" magnetic poles of a magnet _____REPEL_____ each other.

5. "Unlike" magnetic poles _____ATTRACT___ each other.

6. Non-magnetic substances can be _____MAGNETIZED__ by rubbing magnets across them in the same direction.

7. These types of magnets usually don't last very long and are called _____TEMPORARY MAGNETS___ .

8. Magnets which maintain their ability to attact or repel over long periods of time are known as ___PERMANENT__ magnets.

9. The earth has a __MAGNETIC__ ___FIELD___ about it.

10. The magnetized needle in a _____COMPASS___ aligns itself with these fields and points in a _NORTH_-_SOUTH_ direction.

Look at these situations below. Tell if the magnets will attract or repel each other.

11.
| N   S | | N   S | ATTRACT
_____

12.
| S   N | | N   S | REPEL
_____

13.
| S   N | | S   N | ATTRACT
_____

14.
| N   S | | S   N | REPEL
_____

32

Name_____ Date_____

Friendly Physical Science

Lesson 17 Worksheet 1

Please fill in the missing words in each statement below. Refer back to your textbook for help.

1. The movement of ___ELECTRONS__ between atoms or through objects is electricity.

2. __STATIC___ electricity is movement of electrons across relatively short distances.

3. ___CURRENT___ electricity is movement of electrons across long distances.

4. Current electricity is in two forms: ___DIRECT__ current and ___ALTERNATING___ current electricity.

5. Direct current electricity is created by __BATTERIES___ or __SOLAR___ __PANELS___ and flows in ____ONE_____ direction.

6. Alternating current electricity is created by ___GENERATORS_____ and travels in an alternating _____FORWARD_____ and ___REVERSE___ direction.

7. _STATIC_electricity is more of a nuisance, yet must be respected regarding safety issues.

8. Electricity desires to ground into the __EARTH/GROUND___.

9. __LIGHTNING___ rods redirect lightning discharges into the __EARTH/GROUND___ away from building and home structures.

10. ___BATTERIES___ create electricity through the reaction of two unlike __METALS_ and an __ACID___.

11. Electrons travel with ease through ___CONDUCTORS____ and with much greater difficulty through __INSULATORS____.

12. __METALS___, especially copper and aluminum, are very good conductors.

13. Current, measured in __AMPERES/AMPS___, is the__SPEED___ at which electrical charges travel.

14. Voltage, measured in __VOLTS__, is the relative ___STRENGTH__ of the charges.

15. Resistance, measured in ___OHMS__, is the degree to which electrons find it difficult to travel through substances.

16. Watts is a measure of ___POWER__ provided by the electrical circuit and is a derived measurement of __AMPS__ times ____VOLTS_____.

17. Household circuits utilize ____110-120_____ volt __AC_ circuits.

18. Car batteries are usually _____12_____ volt DC circuits.

19. __FUSES__ and ___CIRCUIT BREAKER____ switches allow safe levels of electricity to supply electrical outlets in our homes. in our homes.

Name_____Date_____

Friendly Physical Science

Lesson 17 Worksheet 2

Please tell whether the statement below about electricity is true or false.

1. __FALSE___ Electricity is the flow of protons through substances.

2. __FALSE___ Current electricity is what you see when you receive a shock after sliding your feet across a carpet.

3. __FALSE___ DC electricity comes from generators and what is used in most homes.

4. __TRUE____ Insulators are substances which resist the flow of electricity.

5. ___TRUE____ Lightning is an example of static electricity and can be deadly.

6. ___TRUE____ Batteries work through the chemical reaction of an acid and two unlike metals.

7. ___TRUE____ The speed at which electricity is flowing is known as current and is measured in amperes.

8. ___TRUE____ Resistance to the flow of electricity is measured in ohms.

9. ___FALSE___ Alternating current electricity moves back and forth as it travels away from the battery which produces it.

10. ____TRUE__ Water, held behind a dam, can convert its potential energy into mechanical and ultimately electrical energy through the use of turbines inside the dam.

11. ____TRUE___ Fuses and breaker switches are safety devices which prevent the excess flow of electricity through a circuit.

Name_____ Date_____

Friendly Physical Science

Lesson 18 Worksheet

(Note that Lesson 18 has only one worksheet.)

Please fill in the missing words in each statement below. Refer back to your textbook for help.

1. _____MAGNETIC___ ___FIELDS___ are produced around wires that are carrying electricity.

2. Coils of wires, carrying ___CURRENT__ ___ELECTRICITY__, alongside a soft iron core creates an electromagnet.

3. Electromagnets are ____TEMPORARY____ magnets meaning they only function while electrical current is flowing.

4. A ___SWITCH_____ allows one to control when an electromagnet is functioning and when it is not.

5. The _____POLARITY__ of an electromagnet can be reversed by reversing the flow of electricity.

6. With an electromagnet being controlled by a battery, one simply has to __SWITCH___ the connections on the battery to change the polarity of the magnet.

7. A combination of ___PERMANENT___ magnets and _ELECTROMAGNETS__ with changing polarity allow electric motors to work.

8. Bringing the positive end of an electromagnet near the positive end of a permanent magnet will cause the two magnets to ____REPEL___ each other.

9. The biggest advantage of an electromagnet over a permanent magnet is that electromagnets can be turned __OFF__ and ___ON__ at the user's convenience.

10. ___SOLENOIDS___ are coils of wire which act upon moveable rods found within.

11. Common uses for solenoids include: ____PUMPS_____, _____DOORBELLS_____ and _____STARTERS ON CARS_____.

12. To increase the strength of an electromagnet one can either increase the __NUMBER___ of coils or increase the flow of ___ELECTRICITY__.

13. Look at the diagram below and tell whether the electromagnet within this motor will rotate or stay in this position.

IT WILL ROTATE DUE TO SIMILAR POLARITY OF EACH MAGNET.

Name_____ Date_____

Friendly Physical Science

Lesson 19 Worksheet 1

Please fill in the missing words in each statement below. Refer back to your textbook for help.

1. The source of natural light in our world comes from the _____SUN_____.

2. Man-made light comes from ___LIGHT BULBS_____.

3. Light is defined as the _____VISIBLE SPECTRUM___ of electromagnetic radiation which have the capability of traveling from place to place.

4. Light travels at approximately ___186,000__ miles per second or __669,600,000_____ miles per hour.

5. Light that we can see is part of the ___VISIBLE___ spectrum.

6. Light travels in ___WAVES___ with varying wavelengths.

7. Colors of light are dependent upon the _____WAVELENGTH__ of the light.

8. ___COLORS____ we can observe are the light which has reflected from an object.

9. A ____PRISM_____ can be used to separate light into the spectrum of wavelengths.

10. Refraction is the _____BENDING__ of light as it moves into different substances.

11. ____LENSES_____ are used to bend light rays which enables images to be focused.

12. ____REFLECTION_____ is the bouncing-off of light from a surface.

13. With regard to reflection, the angle of _____INCIDENCE___ equals the angle of ____REFLECTION_____ .

14. Solar energy can be used to create ___DC ELECTRICITY_ through the use of silicon-filled photovoltaic cells.

15. This DC electricity can then be stored in ____BATTERIES____ for later use.

Name_____Date_____

Friendly Physical Science

Lesson 19 Worksheet 2

Examine each diagram below. Label the indicated parts or provide the requested value.

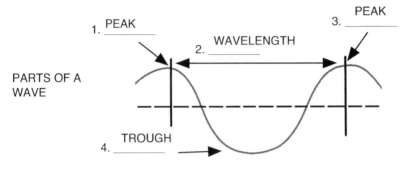

PARTS OF A
WAVE

1. PEAK

2. _____ WAVELENGTH

3. _____ PEAK

4. _____ TROUGH

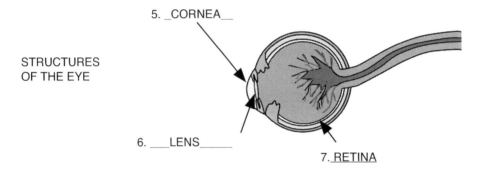

STRUCTURES
OF THE EYE

5. _CORNEA__

6. ___LENS_____

7. RETINA

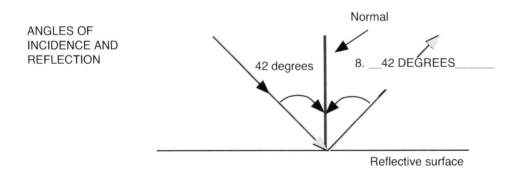

ANGLES OF
INCIDENCE AND
REFLECTION

Normal

42 degrees

8. __42 DEGREES_____

Reflective surface

Name_____ Date_____

Friendly Physical Science

Lesson 20 Worksheet

(Note: there is only one worksheet for Lesson 20)

Please fill in the missing words in each statement below. Refer back to your textbook for help.

1. Sound energy, which travels in ____WAVES_____, is defined as audible changes in ___PRESSURE___ (vibrations) which can travel through a medium such as air.

2. Sounds are described as having a range of __FREQUENCIES__ with high frequencies being ____HIGH____ pitched tones and low frequencies being ____LOW_____ pitched tones.

3. Humans can hear a certain ____RANGE_____ of frequencies while animals can hear frequencies above and below that of humans.

4. Sounds travels much ___SLOWER___ than light only going at ____760_____miles per hour.

5. Light travels __669,600,000____ miles per hour.

6. Sound travels __FASTER____ through water than air and yet, even faster through ___SOLID__ substances.

7. _____ULTRASOUND_____ (very high frequency sound) is used in health diagnosis and for prenatal care.

8. Loudness of sound is measured in ___DECIBLES___.

10. True or False: Loud noises, over long periods of time, generally do no harm to our ears.

                FALSE

Use the chart in your lesson to rate these sounds from softest (1) to loudest (7).

___2__ Quiet office

___3__ Soft radio

___1__   Rustling leaves

___5__ Night club

___7__ Live rock band

___4__ Normal piano practice

___6__ Cymbal crash

Name_____ Date_____

Friendly Physical Science

Lesson 21 Worksheet

(Note: there is only one worksheet for Lesson 21)

Please fill in the missing words in each statement below. Refer back to your textbook for help.

1. All substances contain _____MATTER_____ held in their atoms.

2. There are four phases of matter: _____SOLID_____, _____LIQUID_____, _____GAS_____ and plasma.

3. Solids have the ____LEAST___ amount of energy, liquids have ___MORE ENERGY__, gases even more and plasma the most energy.

4. Adding heat energy to substances allow them to change ____PHASE_____.

5. The temperature at which a solid changes to a liquid is known as the _____MELTING_POINT_____.

6. The temperature at which a liquid changes to a gas is known as the _____VAPOR_____ point or evaporation point.

7. There are three commonly used systems of measuring temperature (heat content) of a substance: ____CELSIUS_____, ___FAHRENHEIT___ and ____KELVIN_____.

8. Zero degrees Kelvin is known as ____ABSOLUTE__ zero where all action of atoms in a substance ____CEASES/STOPS_____.

9. In general, substances ____EXPAND___ when heated and ___CONTRACT___ when cooled.

10. Heat moves through our environment by ____CONDUCTION___, convection or ____RADIATION___.

11. Movement by conduction occurs when heat energy travels __THROUGH__ a substance.

12. Movement by __CONVECTION____ occurs due to the heating of liquids or gases which change density and create movement of those substances to other locations.

13. Movement by ____RADIATION_____ is through travel of infrared radiation and travels in all ___DIRECTIONS___ from the source.

14. Unlike other substances, water _____EXPANDS___ upon freezing.

15. Water has a great capacity to absorb ___HEAT____ without increasing in _____TEMPERATURE_____.

Name_____ Date_____

Friendly Physical Science

Lesson 22 Worksheet

(Note: there is only one worksheet for Lesson 22)

Please fill in the missing words in each statement below. Refer back to your textbook for help.

1. 1. All things, whether living or non-living consist of tiny bits of matter known as _____ATOMS_____.

2. The central portion of an atom is known as the __NUCLEUS__ and it contains subatomic particles known as the _PROTONS__ and the__NEUTRONS___.

3. Circling around the nucleus of the atom are a third type of subatomic particle which are the ___ELECTRONS__.

4. Theories say it is the __ARRANGEMENT_ of the electrons which determines the behavior of various elements on the periodic table.

5. To determine the number of protons or electrons an atom of a particular atom has, one looks for the __ATOMIC NUMBER__ of that element on a periodic table.

6. The electrons are thought to exist in __LAYERS___ around the nucleus of an atom and that there can be no more than __EIGHT ELECTRONS__ on one of these layers.

7. Elements which have their outermost layer of electrons filled are the elements which are very __STABLE__ in their behavior.

8. Elements which have their outermost layers incompletely filled are elements which are very __UNSTABLE__ in their behavior.

9. Elements which are very reactive seek to gain stability by moving or sharing __ELECTRONS__ with neighboring atoms of elements.

10. The family of elements whose atoms have their outer layers of electrons completely filled making their very, very stable is the __NOBLE GAS__ family.

11. Atomic bonds which form between atoms who have transferred electrons from one to another are known as ___IONIC___ bonds.

12. Atomic bonds which form between atoms who are sharing electrons between themselves

are known as ___COVALENT__ bonds.

13. Of the many elements known to man, there are four that are common to all living things.

Those four elements are: __CARBON_C__, ____HYDROGEN__H___, ___OXYGEN

O___ and __NITROGEN N___. Write their element symbols next to their names, too!

14. Of the elements listed below, choose the one that would most likely be the least reactive.

A. Hydrogen

B. Carbon

C. Sodium

D. Neon

15. Of the elements listed below, choose the one that would most likely be the most reactive.

A. Neon

B. Sodium

C. Argon

D. Helium

16. Which subatomic particle is thought to be responsible for an atom's behavior?

A. Proton

B. Neutron

C. Electron

D. Crouton

17. Suppose Atom A desires to get rid of one electron and Atom B is willing to accept that one electron. Together, by moving this electron, they can become a compound which is stable. This type of bond formation where electrons are moved is called a(n)

A. Proton bond

B. Single covalent bond

C. Double covalent bond

D. Ionic bond

E. James bond (LOL)

Tests Answer Key

Lesson # ⟶

	1	2	3	4	5	6	7	8	9	10	11	12	13	14	15	16	17	18	19	20	21	22
1	B	C	B	D	A	A	A	A	A	D	B	A	A	B	B	B	B	B	A	A	A	D
2	B	B	B	C	A	A	B	A	A	A	B	B	C	A	B	A	C	B	A	A	A	D
3	C	B	B	B	B	A	A	B	A	C	B	A	A	A	A	A	A	B	B	B	A	B
4	A	C	C	A	B	A	C	B	C	A	A	A	B	A	C	B	B	A	A	A	D	C
5	C	B	A	C	B	B		C	A	A	D	B	C	A	C	A	C	AB	C	A	C	D
6	B	C	D	A	A	A		A	C	A	C	B	C	A	D	A	B		A	A	A	C
7	D	D	A	D	D	A		A	A	C	A	A	D	A	B	C	D		D	A	A	B
8	A	A	C	B	D	A		A	A		B	C	D	B	A	B	B		A	A	B	B
9	C		C	D	C	B		B	C		B		A	A	B		C		A		A	D
10	D			B	B						C		A	A	A		D					C
11	B			D							D											
12	B																					
13	D																					

Made in United States
Troutdale, OR
09/03/2023